A True
Friend

...Is Someone
Just like You

This book belongs to:
Sara Jilani

Blue Mountain Arts®

Bestselling Titles

By Susan Polis Schutz
To My Daughter with Love on the Important Things in Life
To My Son with Love

By Wally Amos
Be Positive!
The Power of Self-Esteem

By Donna Fargo
I Prayed for You Today
Ten Golden Rules for Living in This Crazy, Mixed-Up World

By Douglas Pagels
100 Things to Always Remember… and One Thing to Never Forget
Every daughter should have a book like this to remind her how wonderful she is
For You, Just Because You're Very Special to Me
May You Always Have an Angel by Your Side
Required Reading for All Teenagers

Anthologies
7 Days to a Positive Attitude
Always Believe in Yourself and Your Dreams
For My Wonderful Mother
For You, My Daughter
God Is Always Watching Over You
Hang In There
Keep Believing in Yourself and Your Dreams
The Love Between a Mother and Daughter Is Forever
There Is Greatness Within You, My Son
Think Positive Thoughts Every Day

A True
Friend

...Is Someone
Just like You

26 Ways That
Girlfriends Are Great!

BJ Gallagher

Blue Mountain Press™
Boulder, Colorado

Dedication

My life and my heart are filled with the gifts my girlfriends have given me — gifts of time, gifts of listening and caring, gifts of encouragement and support, gifts of honesty and compassion, gifts of love and laughter. This book of verse is my "thank you" to my wonderful friends — those with whom I've long since lost touch, those who are with me today, and even those future friends whose acquaintance I have not yet made.

Library of Congress Control Number: 2007903159
ISBN: 978-1-59842-231-3

❚ and Blue Mountain Press are registered in U.S. Patent and Trademark Office. Certain trademarks are used under license.

Printed in China.
First Printing: 2007

♻ This book is printed on recycled paper.

This book is printed on archival quality, white felt, 110 lb. paper. This paper has been specially produced to be acid free (neutral pH) and contains no groundwood or unbleached pulp. It conforms with all the requirements of the American National Standards Institute, Inc., so as to ensure that this book will last and be enjoyed by future generations.

Blue Mountain Arts, Inc.
P.O. Box 4549, Boulder, Colorado 80306

Contents

A True Friend...

A True
Friend

...Is Someone
Just like You

A true friend...

ACCEPTS

you just as you are.

No Strings Attached

No terms and conditions,
   no hesitation or reservations...
that's how you love me.

You embrace me just as I am,
   and I do the same for you.

Mutual trust and respect,
   unconditional love and acceptance,
      commitment to each other's
         well-being...
that's what we have.

In other words,
   we're true friends.

True Friendships Are UNCONDITIONAL...

Unlimited acceptance

Never critical or judging

Communicating with compassion

Open mind, open arms

No strings attached

Dedicated to mutual well-being

Interested in each other's life

Time and attention freely given

Interdependent

Open heart, open home

Never worrying about rejection

Affirming each other's dignity

Loving kindness in all matters

Truth in Advertising

"As is" the sign reads
   in the window of the used car.

"That's me,"
   I think.

My friends see my dings and dents,
   my less-than-perfect paint,
      the subtle signs of wear and tear,
and they know that I am far from perfect.

But they take me anyway,
   just the way I am.

As is.

A true friend...

BELIEVES

in your potential.

Cheering Me On

"Yes, it's a stretch,
but go for it anyway,"
    one friend says.

"You're so talented —
I know you can do it,"
    another joins in.

My friends are cheerleaders —
    a chorus of possibility.
Their words of encouragement
    compete in my mind
        with the sirens of self-doubt
            who sing songs of defeat.

Who do I listen to?
The cheerleaders.

Louder please, Girls,
I'm feeling a little shaky today.

It's Nice to Know
I'm Not Alone

It's so easy for women
    to slip into self-doubt
        and feelings of inadequacy.
After all,
we shoulder a lot of responsibilities —
    being supportive of our mates,
    nurturing our children,
    staying in touch with extended family,
    holding down jobs
    while holding down the fort at home.

No wonder we sometimes feel
    anxious,
        exhausted,
            and insecure,
        as we second-guess ourselves.

We need to know
    we're not alone.
We need to hear
    that other women
        share our experiences.

"You're doing great!"
   never sounded so sweet
      as when coming from the lips
         of another woman.
She understands;
   she's been there, done that.
She gets it —
   she gets *me*.

We take turns
   encouraging,
      supporting,
         and cheering each other on.

We learn to do it for ourselves, too.
Just reach right over your shoulder, Girl,
   and pat yourself on the back.

You're terrific,
   and you and I both know it.

A true friend...

COMFORTS

you when you're sad.

That Which Is Shareable
Is Bearable

I've learned that
    if I can share my troubles,
        I can bear them.

It's true.
It makes me feel better to have you around
    when I'm down.
Your presence reassures me;
    your listening soothes me;
        your hug consoles me.
It's nice to have company —
    even if it's in the pits.

I don't need cheery platitudes of
    positive thinking
        or a booming bravado urging me to
            "cheer up."

No...
What I really need right now
    is just the comfort of your company...

...and maybe a little chocolate.

True Friends Provide
COMFORT...

Caring companionship

Open arms

Much love

Food that nourishes and soothes

Ongoing support

Really good ears for listening

Trust and confidence

Wonder-full

Sometimes I am a mystery
   to myself...
"Why am I depressed?"
   I sometimes ask.
"I just burst into tears for no reason,"
   I complain.
"I don't know why I feel this way,"
   I wonder.
"Why am I here —
what's the meaning of my life?"
   I ask myself.

To be a woman is to be a mystery,
but it helps to have a friend
who encourages me to explore
   what intrigues me,
inquire into
      what puzzles me,
and seek answers to
      what vexes me.

Women wonder
   and women *are* a wonder!

We are wonder-full.

A true friend...

DELIGHTS

in your successes.

An All-Weather Friend

It's easy to be my friend
when I'm having a hard time,
   not doing so well.
Some friends hold out a helping hand,
offer me tea with a bit of advice,
and deep down inside
feel just a teensy bit superior.
But those foul-weather friends
   disappear like clouds
      when my fortunes improve.

But you, dear friend,
you're here in foul weather *and* fair.
You delight when I'm on top of the world,
   flying high, reveling in success.

You know that my achievement
   doesn't diminish yours
and there's plenty of success
   to go around.

True Friends Know the Real Meaning of SUCCESS...

Self-acceptance and self-love

Unlimited happiness and fulfillment

Contribution and service to others

Commitment to personal
   and professional relationships

Energy and enthusiasm for life

Sharing the journey with friends
   and loved ones

Spiritual growth and serenity

Celebrate!

"Good news!"
    you announce happily
    when I answer the phone.

We squeal like a couple of schoolgirls
    about your latest achievement.

"Where shall we go to celebrate?"
    I ask.
"Pizza and beer
or steak and champagne?
    You choose.
        I'm buying!"

I'm as happy for you as I would be
    for my own success,
for joy multiplies
    when it's shared.

And next time, perhaps
    it will be me with the good news.

That's the whole reason
to have good news,
    isn't it?
So we can celebrate
    with a true friend.

A true friend...

EMPATHIZES

with your struggles.

Sister Struggler

I know you can't feel my pain;
   no one can.
My suffering is unique,
   as is yours and everyone else's, too.

But it helps to know
   that you can imagine my pain
      as I struggle with problems.
It helps to know that you've struggled, too,
   though our struggles may not be the same.

Thank you, Sister Struggler.
I can't feel your pain,
   but I can feel your love.

S.O.S.
(Sharing Our Struggles)

We all have difficulties,
   challenges,
      and problems to bear.
We can't ask others
   to take them from us,
      for they already have their own.

But we *can* ask them
   to help us —
      to share our burdens and trials.

And we, in turn,
   can do the same for them.

As friends, we shift and share
our struggles and troubles —
   lightening the burden
      by lifting the load
         off each other's shoulders.

Our synergy multiplies our strength,
and together
   we can handle
      almost anything.

A true friend...

FORGIVES

you when you hurt
her feelings.

Mea Culpa

That old song is true:
"You often hurt the ones you love."

The careless comment,
    the commitment not kept,
       the promise broken.
How could I have done such a dumb thing?

Please forgive me —
    I didn't mean to hurt you.

You sigh and nod
    as you look at me with loving eyes.
Your hug tells me that you understand.
We smile at each other,
    wiping away a tender tear.

And we move on...

Until next time,
    when perhaps it's my turn
       to sigh and forgive.

A true friend...

GIVES you

time and attention.

Interest Compounded Daily

Our friendship
is like a bank account —
   growing in proportion
   to the amount of interest we pay.

A mutual fund,
we might call it —
   both of us enriched
   by our investment
   in each other.

Our assets include:
   compassion and caring,
      love and laughter,
         giving and gratitude.
We are wealthy
   beyond our wildest dreams.

True Friends Are
GENEROUS...

Giving without conditions

Eager to help in any way possible

Never keeping score

Embracing opportunities to share
   abundantly

Recognizing that it is the giver
   who is most enriched

Opening one's heart anytime, anywhere

Understanding that what goes around,
   comes around

Sharing time, attention, and love

Got a Minute?

"Got a minute?"
I ask.

"For you, always,"
you reply.

That's one of the things
I love most about you.

When I need a minute... or ten,
you always say, "Sure."

When I need a place to cry,
you make your shoulder available.

When I want to bend someone's ear,
you lend me yours.

You give me time,
attention,
listening,
and love.

What more could I ask
of a friend?

A true friend...

HUGS you
...often.

A Call to Arms

Hug therapy...

Safe,
inexpensive,
readily available,
needs no instruction manual,
proven effective,
guaranteed to lift spirits
    and warm the heart.

I'm having new business cards printed:

    "Hug Therapist."

Hugs Unlimited

How do I hug thee?
Let me count the ways...

- ☙ a happy hug when I meet you for lunch
- ☙ a comforting hug when you're sad or upset
- ☙ a congratulatory hug on your latest success
- ☙ a joyful hug when we get together for
   the holidays
- ☙ a birthday hug on your special day
- ☙ a "good-bye for now" hug whenever
   we part
- ☙ a happy surprise hug when we bump into
   each other unexpectedly

...and the list goes on,
because, you know...
it's impossible to have too many hugs.

A true friend...

INSPIRES you

to do your best.

Score: Love/Love

I've been told that in sports
it's good to play
with a partner who's better than you.
It improves your game
    and makes you play your best.

I feel that way
    about us.
Having you as my friend
    makes me do my best
        to rise to any occasion.

In our game of friendship
there are no losers —
    it's always win/win.

Go for It!

You remind me that
life is like a fabulous buffet
   spread out before me.

You encourage me
   to help myself
to as much as my plate
   can possibly hold...
to savor the sights and sounds,
   the smells and tastes,
      the sensation of experiences
      each and every day.

You inspire me
   to go for it —
flat out,
   pedal to the metal,
      full tilt.

Now, that's how to live!

You're Such a Good Influence on Me

You're like my coach,
    my cheerleader,
        and my marching band —
all rolled into one person.

Your confidence in me
    gives me confidence in myself.

I can never fail
    with you in my corner.
I go for the goal
    because you've got my back.
I give it all I've got
    because you would expect nothing less.

Having you as my friend
    makes me a winner.

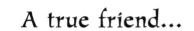

A true friend...

JUST

loves you.

Grace-full

Dearest friend,
you've shown me
that you love me
not for what I do,
    but for who I am.

You've taught me that
I'm not a *human doing* —
    I'm a human being.

Your friendship isn't earned —
    it's a gift,
        freely given.

I'm deeply grateful...
    and grace-full.

Thank you.

A true friend...

KEEPS

your secrets.

Sacred Trusts

Some things are too important,
   too sensitive, too painful,
      too delicate
to be shared with the whole world.

Dreams, hopes, fears,
memories, fantasies, heart's desires...
These are soul secrets —
   sacred trusts —
safe only with a bosom buddy
who will hold them gently
with love and respect
   in the confines of her heart.

Thank you for being my confidante,
   my trusted friend,
      my secret agent.

A true friend...

LISTENS

with her heart.

Heart Sounds

Dearest friend,
you listen not just with your ears,
but with your heart,
   your mind,
      your soul,
         your entire being.

You listen between the lines —
paying attention
to what I *don't* say,
   as well as what I do.

You genuinely want to know
   what's going on with me.

You listen
   to the language
      of my heart.

A true friend...

MAKES

you want to be

a better person.

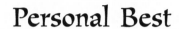

Personal Best

I don't compete with you —
  I compete with myself.

But you play an important role —
  inspiring me,
    motivating me,
      being a great example.

I work harder to close the gap
between who I am today
  and who I want to be someday.

Your love and support
help fuel my quest
  to achieve my personal best in life.

If they ever held
an Olympic competition for friendships,
  ours would win the gold for sure!

Inspired Friendship

You inspire me to be
   more thoughtful,
   more patient,
   more compassionate.

You motivate me,
   not with scolds or lectures,
but with the quiet example
   you set.

I look up to you;
   I respect you;
      I admire your gifts and your grace.

I love the way you walk your talk
   and live your beliefs.

Your integrity,
   character,
      and authenticity
make me grateful
that you're my friend.

A true friend...

NEVER
JUDGES you.

Evidence of Friendship

Judgments and opinions
are all around me —
some spoken, some silent,
but nonetheless evident
in a frown, a sigh, or a raised eyebrow.

My life is full of judges and juries.
Thankfully, you're not one of them.

To what do I owe
    your absence of evaluation and
        criticism?
How can I explain
    your unconditional positive regard —
        your complete acceptance of me
            as I am?

The verdict is in...
    Motive: love.
    Opportunity: plenty.
    Sentence: a lifetime of friendship.

A true friend...

OCCASIONALLY DISAPPOINTS

you because

she's human, too.

Perfectly Imperfect

I'm disappointed, annoyed, sad.
"How could she?" I cry.

But then I remind myself:

She's not perfect, not infallible,
    not superwoman.
She's only human —
    she makes mistakes,
        forgets things,
            does or says things
                she later regrets.

Well, thank goodness for that!
If she were perfect,
    I couldn't be her friend
        because my own imperfection
            would be too painful to bear.

Yes, we are quite the pair —
    perfectly imperfect.

Expectations

I've learned the hard way that
   expectations often lead
      to resentments.

A friend disappoints me,
   and I'm hurt and angry.
Resentment bubbles up inside,
   and I have a bitter taste in my mouth.
I want to complain and protest
   the disappointment I've suffered.

So, how long do I carry
my disappointment and resentment?

Not long,
   if I'm smart.

For holding on to a resentment
   is like carrying rocks
     in my stomach —
weighing me down
   and making me sick.

I must let it go —
   forgive and move on —
     for my own sake
    as well as hers.

And I must remember
to let go of expectations, too,
   and love my friends
   just as they are —
     not how I expect them to be.

A true friend...

POINTS OUT

your good qualities

when you forget.

Fill in the Blanks

My mind is a mismatch detector.
I always notice what's wrong
    and overlook what's right.

My memory is faulty;
    my mirror is flawed;
I'm my own worst critic.

Then I hear your voice:
"I love the way you do that."
"You're so clever with these things."
"I wish I was good at that, like you are."
"You're so: ☐ smart
            ☐ creative
            ☐ resourceful
            ☐ (fill in the blank)."

You remind me
    when I forget the good stuff.
Thanks, dear friend, I needed that!

A true friend...

QUESTIONS you
when you're about to do
something really dumb.

Second Opinion

"**A**re you sure you want to do that?"
    you ask me.
"What are your other options?"
    you query kindly.
"Would you like me to help you think this
    through?" you offer generously.
"Maybe you want to get another opinion,"
    you suggest supportively.

Some of my friends just go along to get along,
    saying "yes" to avoid conflict
        or hurt feelings.
But *true* friends, like you,
    ask courageous questions,
    speaking up when you're concerned
        for my well-being.

Thank you for all the times
    you've saved me from myself!

If My Friends
Won't Tell Me,
Who Will?

I depend on you to give me
the feedback I need...
   to make good decisions,
   to change course
     when I'm on the wrong path,
   to say I'm sorry
     when the fault is mine.

Thank goodness I have you
   to keep an eye out for me.

I can't tell you how much
   I value your insight and honesty.

Two heads really *are*
   better than one...
especially when one of those heads
   is yours.

A true friend...

RESPECTS

your boundaries.

Limits, Not Limitations

You and I both understand
that the time and energy
we have to give
   are not unlimited.

You support me
in sticking to my priorities,
   and I do the same for you.

You've taught me that
if I don't take care of myself first,
   I can't take care of anyone else.

I used to think that
   "too much of a good thing
      is a good thing,"
but I've learned that it's not.
All good things —
   like good friends —
      have limits.

Our healthy boundaries
   keep our friendship healthy.

A true friend...

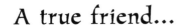

SHARES her hopes
and fears with you.

A Jewel Box

My heart is a jewel box
where I carefully stash
    the gems of hopes and dreams
        you share with me.
They shine and sparkle
    in the light of possibility
when we look at them together.

Your fears are in there, too,
rough rocks that I wrap in velvet concern
to keep them from scratching or damaging
    the bright hopes.

They're all in there together —
    hopes and fears, coexisting side by side.
Hopes to be cherished,
fears to be respected —
    both true, both real, both valuable.
I keep them safe
    in the jewel box of my heart.

A true friend...

TELLS you
the truth.

Mirror Image

My friends are mirrors.
They show me to myself.
They reflect what they see
     so that I can see it, too.

The good,
     the bad,
          and the ugly.
It's all there.

But my friends' love enables me
     to see the truth
          through clear eyes,
without having to avert my gaze
     in shame or guilt.

Mirror, mirror on the wall,
     who's my best friend,
          after all?

True Friends Are
AUTHENTIC...

Aware

Understanding

Tactful

Honest

Empathetic

Natural

Tuned in

Intimate

Caring

Loving Truth-Teller

Experience has taught me that
   honesty without love
   is brutality,
and
   love without honesty
   is just sentimentality.

It's both I need —
   honesty with love —
and that's what you give me.

Thanks, dear friend,
   I need that.

A true friend...

UNDERSTANDS

you, even when you don't
understand yourself.

Ice-Cream Hangover

"I can't believe it," I groan.
"I ate a whole pint of ice cream last night!
 I'll never lose weight... It's hopeless."

"It's not what you're eating," she replies.
"It's what's eating you.
 What was going on
 before the ice cream?"

"I don't know..." I say.

"Why don't you spend some time
 thinking and writing about it?"
     she suggests.
"There's a message in the ice cream.
 It's a gift.
 What's it trying to tell you?"

The gift of the ice cream...
     what a great way to think about it!

I love the way you help me
     understand myself.

In the Fishbowl

Why is it that it's so easy to see
what someone else needs to do
    but we can't see what *we* need to do?

The solutions to others' problems
seem blindingly obvious,
    while our own dilemmas befuddle us.

We're like fish in a fishbowl —
    we can't see the water
    because we're *in* it.

But others looking in from the outside
    can see the water quite clearly.

I'm lucky to have friends like you —
   who see me and my life
   from a clear perspective.

You help me understand myself
   when my thinking
   becomes cloudy.

You call me on my nonsense
   when I'm fooling myself.

I'm swimming safer in life
   thanks to your loving perspective.

A true friend...

VALUES your ideas
and opinions.

Yours for the Asking

"What do you think?" she asks,
    and unlike some people,
    she really means it.

I value her counsel
    and she values mine.

We bounce ideas
back and forth —
building on each other's thoughts,
    growing,
        flowing,
            thinking,
and often laughing —
    enjoying the process
    as much as the result.

"What do you think?" I ask.
No telling where
that question will take us!

Mining for Gold

All ideas
are not created equal.

Some are brilliant —
        others not so much.
And I hate to admit it,
        but a few
        are even crazy!

As my friend,
   you help me
      sort out my ideas —
separating the bright ones
from the dim,
   the inspired
   from the dull,
      the sublime
      from the ridiculous...

Your perspective is helpful;
your insight is on target.

Thank you
for helping me find
my fourteen-carat nuggets
   amidst the fool's gold.

A true friend...

WILL DO

anything she can
to help you.

Sweet Offering

"Is there anything I can do?"
You've asked me
    that sweet question
        many times over the years.

Your heart,
your mind,
your schedule,
your home,
your pocketbook
    are always open to me
        if I need them.

Sometimes there's nothing
you can do...
    and we both know it.

But still you offer.
And in your offering
    I find everything I need.

True Friends Offer
a HELPING HAND...

Hearing distress in a friend's voice

Expressing emotional support

Listening for clues on how best to help

Providing practical assistance

Inquiring into what's needed most

Never violating a friend's dignity

Going to any lengths

Helping by simply being present

Asking without making assumptions

Noticing when your help isn't helping

Delineating healthy boundaries

How Can I Ever Thank You?

What would I do without you?
You're always there for me,
    in good times and in bad...

Cheering me on
    when I'm discouraged;
offering suggestions
    when I get lost;
nudging me gently
    when I feel lazy;
extending your hand
    when I need some help;
lending an ear
    while I whine and complain;
sharing your shoulder
    when I just want to cry;
giving me a big "thumbs up"
    when I make good progress.

Words seem inadequate
    to express my love and gratitude —
        so I hope you can hear
            the whispers of my heart...

"Thanks, friend."

A true friend...

'XTENDS

you the benefit
of the doubt.

Doubtless

I forget to return her calls sometimes.
I'm late for our lunch together.
I get lost on my way
    to our designated meeting place.

She doesn't get upset —
    she knows I love her.
She tolerates my mistakes
    with patience and grace.
She knows my intentions are good,
    though sometimes
        my behavior falls short.

My friend is generous.
She always gives me
    the benefit of the doubt.

True Friends Enjoy
GIVING BACK...

Going to great lengths to reciprocate

Insight into each other's wants and needs

Vested in mutual health and happiness

Interested in joint love and respect

Never being selfish

Growing by giving

Being supportive, not condescending

Accepting that we all need one another

Committed to open, loving communication

Keeping a healthy balance of give and take

Intent Versus Impact

Most people have a double standard:
    they judge themselves
    by their *intentions*,
        but they judge others
        by their *actions*.

True friends aren't like that.
They give each other
credit for good intentions,
    just as they do themselves.

As my friend,
you trust that my intent is always good,
    even if the *impact* isn't.
You understand that there's often a gap
    between intent and impact.

Thank you for being wise and insightful.
From your example
I've learned how to extend others
    the benefit of the doubt.

You're my teacher
    as well as my friend.

A true friend...

YEARNS

to hear from you

when you're away.

Absence Makes
Our Friendship Fonder

Time goes by...
Friends come and go
    just as the seasons do.
But *true* friends come and never go,
    though time and distance
        may sometimes
            keep us apart.

I miss you when you're away.
My days are busy and full, as usual,
but still...
    something's missing.

I long to hear your voice on the phone
    or see your face as you walk through
        my door.

For when we connect,
    time and distance seem to melt away.
We pick up right where we left off...
    and it's as if you were never gone at all.

True Friends Bridge the Gap Created by LONG DISTANCE...

Listening for the phone

Opening my mailbox eagerly each afternoon

Noticing how much I miss you

Going about my day wondering how
your day is going

Delighting in your messages from afar

Interested in your adventures

Seeing a movie that I know you'd like

Taking time to note things I want to tell you

Anticipating the catching up we'll do

Never forgetting about you

Counting the days

Eagerly awaiting your return

Faraway Friend

My friend is out of town
and I miss her.
I think about her and wonder...

Is she having a good time?
Is the trip going well?
What's she seeing and doing?
Who's she meeting?

I can't wait for a full report
when she gets back...

She'll regale me with stories of
sights and sounds,
people and places,
antics and adventures,
food and fun.

A true friend...

Z INGS with joy
because you're friends.

All of the Above!

Who knows why
   I love being friends with you?
Is it your energy?
   Your curiosity?
   Your sense of humor?
   Your talent and creativity?
Yes, all of the above.
I love the way we connect —
   we just click.

I know you feel the same about me —
   I can just feel it.
A mutual admiration society,
   that's what we have.
Why is it so special with you
   and not with someone else?

I don't know — don't have to.
I just accept the joy
   for what it is...
      gratefully.

About the Author

BJ Gallagher is an author, speaker, storyteller, and poet. She believes that poetry is the language of the heart, and the heart is where we hold our friends — like precious gems in a jewel box.

BJ has written thirteen other books, including the international bestseller *A Peacock in the Land of Penguins.* She is also the author of *YES Lives in the Land of NO, Everything I Need to Know I Learned from Other Women,* and *Friends Are Everything.*

BJ lives in a cozy cottage in Los Angeles with some of her favorite friends — the four-legged, furry variety. For more information about BJ, visit her website: *www.womenneed2know.com* or contact her at *bbjjgallagher@aol.com.*